The Unbeliever

THE BRITTINGHAM PRIZE IN POETRY

The University of Wisconsin Press Poetry Series
Ronald Wallace, General Editor

Places/Everyone • Jim Daniels
C. K. Williams, Judge, 1985

Talking to Strangers • Patricia Dobler
Maxine Kumin, Judge, 1986

Saving the Young Men of Vienna • David Kirby
Mona Van Duyn, Judge, 1987

Pocket Sundial • Lisa Zeidner
Charles Wright, Judge, 1988

Slow Joy • Stefanie Marlis
Gerald Stern, Judge, 1989

Level Green • Judith Vollmer
Mary Oliver, Judge, 1990

Salt • Renée Ashley
Donald Finkel, Judge, 1991

Sweet Ruin • Tony Hoagland
Donald Justice, Judge, 1992

The Red Virgin: A Poem of Simone Weil • Stephanie Strickland
Lisel Mueller, Judge, 1993

The Unbeliever • Lisa Lewis
Henry Taylor, Judge, 1994

THE

UNBELIEVER

Lisa Lewis

The University of Wisconsin Press

The University of Wisconsin Press
114 North Murray Street
Madison, Wisconsin 53715

3 Henrietta Street
London WC2E 8LU, England

2   4   5   3   1

PRINTED IN THE UNITED STATES OF AMERICA

Library of Congress Cataloging-in-Publication Data
Lewis, Lisa, 1956–
The unbeliever / Lisa Lewis.
72 p.   cm. — (Brittingham prize in poetry)
ISBN 0-299-14400-3   ISBN 0-299-14404-6 (pbk.)
1. Title   II. Series.
PS3562.E9535U53   1994
811'.54—dc20   94-10661

For my mother

. . . And there's one other experience I want you to have. And when I tell you to wake up, to wake up from the neck up. Your body will remain sound asleep. Now, it will be hard to awaken from the neck up, but you can do it. Now, soon you'll begin awakening from the neck up. Now, don't be scared, because your body is sound asleep. Take all the time necessary to wake up from the neck up. It's hard work, but you can do it. . . .

Now your head is beginning to wake up. Your eyes are beginning to open. . . . You can do it. And maybe your body, still sound asleep, will be that of a little girl. You are slowly awakening from the neck up. Your eyes are beginning to flutter open. As you lift your head, your neck unfreezes. . . .

Lift the head and see me.

Is your head awake?

—Milton Erickson

. . . And if for him the law guarantees an increment of pleasure, and power, it would be good to uncover what this implies about his desire—*he seems to get more sexual satisfaction from making laws than love*—and about the eternally abortive, reductive, diversionary effects that this extra satisfaction for the father and the paternal function has upon the little girl . . .

—Luce Irigaray

CONTENTS

IV

ACKNOWLEDGMENTS

Missouri Review: Red Ribbon; The Innocent Embrace; Revisions
River Styx: Night Ride
Western Humanities Review: The Accident
Pequod: Eclipse
Fine Madness: The Mirror; The Visitor
Poetry East: The Urinating Man; Quadriplegics; Genesis
Agni: True Confessions
Antioch Review: The Heart And The Symbol
Graham House Review: Trains
American Poetry Review: Bridget; February; Responsibility
"The Urinating Man" was reprinted in *Best American Poetry 1993.*

I

Night Ride

The employees of the Orbit Company Warehouse Store are lining up in the
  parking lot,
A rhumba line of mid-size Chryslers and Chevrolets swaying over speed
  bumps,
When a boy at the corner bus-stop chokes on bubblegum.
Another kid—his little brother?—smacks him on the back, high as he can
  reach;
He has to swing his arm as if winding up for a pitch.
The gum's stuck in there good, too, a hard raspberry stretching the throat's
  rings.
The last strong rays of afternoon glisten in spit
Thin as egg white on the boy's chin; inside the plexiglass bus-stop shelter, the
  company nurse
Holds a torn copy of *People* magazine to shield her eyes.
She'll have to ride long after dark to get to her house across town.
The boys have taken her bus before, but for all she knows they ride the loop
  around
To the new, spiffier subdivisions, the swimming pools locked behind iron
  lace;
For all she knows, they ride the loop all night,
Trying to map its elastic shape like the body of a cartoon dog,
Familiar and almost lovable, a little frightening too.
Tonight the bus is late, and when the boys get on, she thinks
They look bright but unkempt, the older one's hair stuck like stamps to his
  forehead;
And the fingertips pressed to the point of the throat,
A funny gesture, testing for pain, something about *touch*.

A bus shoves two slender cones of converging light,
Low-beam, towards oncoming traffic. You're driving
A Cadillac, skim milk with sweet butter seats and a cassette deck
Turned up wide-ass open. What if you decide to follow the bus you saw the
  boys climb on?—
Closing in by car-lengths, you couldn't tell if the one whose hands fluttered
Was playing or dying, his back turned toward you,
The crossed straps of his overalls dropped around his hips.
You might be genuinely concerned about the kid's well-being,

Or maybe you were reminded of something, the way the smaller boy kept watching
The traffic, and tried to shield the face of his friend from the stark impersonal sunglassed drivers
Idly turning their heads like birds above the hoods of their sedans. . . .

The air, acrid and rippling with pavement steam;
The slow leak of night into day like ink into clear water;
The horse and rider on a gravel road where it opens onto a highway.
You remember the horse getting nervous, its head held stiffly.
You watched foam like clabbered cream form between the horse's thighs
As the girl turned him around and around, her skinny arm hauling the rein to the side,
The horse's neck curved to the arc of the circle, always the same one.
You remember thinking she looked afraid, and you wondered why
She had to ride the horse at nightfall onto the highway; the sharp *tock* of his shoes on asphalt
Shocked him through his whole body. The girl sat on his back like a board.
He wouldn't go. So—maybe she'd seen it on tv—she made a blindfold
Of her sweater around his loaf of a head, tucking the arms in,
And rode him again for the road and the darkness.
A truck showed up, a shoebox at the vanishing point;
A tremor rolled over the horse's knees like stockings.
Then the muscles of his buttocks were pumping him backwards,
The girl sticking to his slick neck, her face blank with helplessness,
As if she'd just been thrust tail-first through a trap-door
Into deep space—
And below, the invisible paths of birds. Their eyes, pellets, see almost everything. . . .

You think of a gray parrot trying his stubby wings, cobblestone feathers
A fast blur on either side of the crabbed head; the beak opens
Enough to see the hard, fat tongue, its tip.
This parrot, which you don't remember
You saw in a filthy downtown pet shop, made you foolishly apprehensive,
As if he might lift off in your face with a sound like an overcoat shaken out a window,
As if from that moment you would be lessened, no longer to count
Yourself among the ranks of the relatively moral, who are *doing all they can.*
You believe something in the pecan-sized brain charging the body of the parrot
Has found you out—your bland habits of observation,
Your odd detachment in the face of pain, your lack of relief

4

When it all turns out to be another cosmic joke, and luck picks up
The dropped rein, or dislodges the chunk of bubblegum wedged in the c...
   trachea.
You glance over as a car pulls beside you; I'm inside, and you
Don't know me, but you recognize the look on my face and speed up, with a
   new story, this one
About you: you are a policeman's wife, and one night your husband the
   sergeant brings home
A teen-aged girl in a bikini and one of his blue shirts.
A boyfriend left her on the beach, she hitchhiked, slept,
And woke with someone's hands in her crotch, his wooly mouth at her face.
Lucky for her, the jerk's numb-nuts when she's conscious —
Your husband says, and you make her a bed on the sofa, in the heat a sheet
   and pillow.
You think she looks hard to hurt; you don't trust her.
All night you watch from an armchair just inside your room.
Lights shine on her sunburned face, but she's tired and doesn't wake,
And you have to see.

The Urinating Man

ne of Erickson's patients phoned him in the middle of the night.
C.   . college professor, had come to Erickson with a simple question:
Why w   the orgasmic response of the human male referred to as
   "ejaculation"?
The man had a wife and two children, so Erickson asked him
What happened to *him* when he and his wife made love.
After a while, said the man, the semen flows out of your penis,
Just as if you were urinating.
Questioning revealed the man had wet the bed till he was twelve;
He had learned a penis was for peeing, and that's what he did.
But it was not Erickson's method to "probe" or deliver "insights."
He instructed the man on ways to enhance the feeling in his penis.
He was to handle the various parts and identify their sensations;
He was to drill at exciting himself while restraining the pee-flow of semen.
After a month the phone rang at midnight. "I did it," the man said.
He had had an ejaculation, in bed with his wife, for the first time.
He called again at one-thirty. "I did it again," he said.

I have never before repeated the story of the urinating man;
I have never paraphrased it, aloud or on paper.
The story of the urinating man is funny but frightening too—
To think of the pathetic egotism and embarrassment
Keeping him for most of his life from finding out why
The world spoke with confidence of geysers and the best he knew was a
   trickle.
Certainly he was "functional"—though his wife told Erickson later
Their sex life had suddenly improved the night he made the phone call—
The content of which, and its preceding therapy, forever kept secret from
   her.
Perhaps there is actually reason to fear, the things we fear are wrong with us
Are really wrong—
The assurances we assuage ourselves with
Are injunctions lest it be found out we *do* do things wrong,
We *are* secretly different from everyone else on earth.
The urinating man had told himself he was fine as he was.
He had fathered two children, so things were obviously "working";
His wife had never mentioned anything unusual.
The miracle is that the man *ever* asked his question,

6

Giving up a lifetime of carefully tested explanations
That must finally have begun to grow thin.

People are afraid of keeping secrets between their legs.
They are afraid to look there with a strong light
And then have nothing to compare with.
Some of them suspect that what is wrong with them
Is that they are sure something's wrong:
If they went to someone knowledgeable, like a doctor, a therapist,
And he or she said, absolutely nothing's wrong
And turned with that smirk doctors half-conceal
When a patient's worries have just been revealed as groundless,
How would they learn what the urinating man had to learn? —
How to make himself feel better without telling himself anything;
How to take himself into his hands.
It would be better to have someone make you do a thing like that,
Someone you knew could make you do it, like a doctor,
And would make you do it for a good reason,
Like a famous doctor; and money would change hands,
The idea being that the money would change hands.
If you had been one of Erickson's patients, say one of the last ones,
In the seventies, you would have contracted him for his services.
It might have meant his answering the phone at midnight
And again at one a.m. — and he was old, lamed all his life with polio.
You would pay to tell him intimate things,
The old, lame man; and then, because he was the doctor,
And paid to speak, he'd tell you something.

Trains

I go to bed early. I have to get up.
I have to teach "The Dead" at 8 in a classroom with a view
Of a park bench, a backhoe, and a drainage ditch;
Half my class will not show up, maybe because
I'm a lousy teacher, maybe because the November sun,
A winter-pale Texan flashing a belt buckle,
Lounges behind the clouds all day, and the buzz
Of fluorescence over our heads reminds us of nothing
About Gretta and the boy who died of love.
Some of us will try anyway to talk about metaphor,
Me because it's my habit, my dubious "profession,"
Always causing me some kind of trouble, like Christmas,
When I visit home and use my critical skills
To sink the Love Boat until my stepfather—
Who *likes* a little T and A—gets so pissed off
He has to go for a drive, alone except for the fifth of vodka
Shoved under the front seat. In the morning at my podium
I'll be thinking of metaphors for the students' wandering talk—
Maybe *trains moving slowly the far side of the freeway,*
What I hear when I wake up, leaden, in the middle of the night,
Three hours left of the sleep I believe I deserve.
The buzz of the lights will be just like
The bumping rumble of boxcars over the tracks,
Some of the old ones marked "Virginian," "Norfolk & Western."
My grandfather worked those lines even longer
Than he was married to Greta Ardella Musselman Thomas—
Who was dark and clever in the life she lived hard,
Years before my birth. Hissing through the warehouse district,
Locomotives remind me of lights, floodlights outside my window
In the house where I grew up: my grandmother—
I called her Nana, so for years she bragged
"That's what German children call *their* grandmothers,"
I've never learned if she was right—
Nana liked to hear noises in the night and track them down
With the floodlight; she liked to be afraid.
I was easy to scare too; I'd hang onto her housedress,
Feeling her body stiffen a little, like an animal,
While she looked all over the cone of light—

My swingset at the top of the slope,
Where once it turned over on me, skinning my knees;
Branches of dogwood, thick, snaky, black
And elaborate, crowding into the squat trunk
So someone could still be hiding there, you couldn't see all the way;
The square plot of peony, old-fashioned rose,
Poppy, a hundred grape hyacinths and buttercups
I imagined winking like fireflies in the untrimmed border grass;
Forsythia shrubs like beehives or hogans, big enough
To crawl inside; the dog pen, where the lonely white terrier
Peered, nose and eyes between canvas flaps my grandfather nailed
To the front of her shingled house; hedges, raspberry brambles,
Path into secret blackness where the light died out
Over twisted apple trees; the rusted-out '56 Cadillac
Promised for when I turned sixteen
Because we were the same age and Nana couldn't really imagine
Me getting my license. . . .
She looked all over, not losing interest, not reassured
The way I was in a flash, so all I could do was look up at her,
Her gray eyes quaking a tiny bit, the irises.
Then we'd hear the trains shuffling
At least a mile away, sometimes the whistle
For a dangerous crossing, sometimes answered by a braying mule
Nana said it wasn't legal to keep inside city limits,
And the piercing whistle, the clicking rails,
Would sound a lot closer than a mile away,
So I'd believe I could see the train, the headlight like the full moon,
Boxcars in our back alley, elephant shapes just visible
Beyond the picket gate. Nana and I would be ready
For my grandfather to come home, but he worked second shift,
I'd always be asleep. Mornings I'd see his striped jacket
Slung over the back of a chair; I liked the smell,
The smell of machines, darkness, and oil, and cinders.
Once Grandfather lifted me up to the steps of a fueling engine,
My baby feet in their cute white shoes touching
The metal grating, and I don't remember
What made me start screaming like a spoiled little bitch
Right in front of the engineers, who laughed,
But Grandfather didn't; later Nana whipped me with a switch
She cut from a peach tree that never did set blooms—
Where we lived, snows were light but early and late too.
Sap burned into the skin on the backs of my legs
And I screamed that much louder then;

Grandfather put on his jacket and went out for a walk.
There was no way he could know how wrong I'd someday think
He was—leaving me to scenes he couldn't watch—
Or that I'd later lie awake to place blame
Like a plastic wreath at the foot of the solemn monument
The past erects to itself in private. I stumble into the bathroom
And twist the hot tap on; when the water hits cold porcelain,
Steam streaks the mirror. It's a kind of physical property
Not to be had with false tears or real tears, wisdom, obsession,
Cleverness, pure chance, honesty, passion:
Trains are nudging one another
Straight from the low blue mountains of Virginia
To the raped flat strands of the Texas Gulf Coast and back;
They are sending one another coded messages.
And at this very moment I am finding a book
The cats must've pushed into the bathtub, I am opening it
To the first page, I am brushing up on the story
I teach in the morning; it won't be much longer before I go in—
A neighbor's backyard rooster crows, anachronistic in the city—
And here's a pencil for me to take notes with.

Quadriplegics

In the big Sunday paper every story is about death.
A conventional lament for young life sacrificed
Or rendered so difficult—permanently—
The victim's continued existence becomes heroic:
The football star who broke his neck on the playing field
Has persevered, and though his every bodily need
Is tended by another person, he maneuvers a stick between his teeth
To finish college and ultimately start a business;
His is the lead human interest story in the "Lifestyles" section.

But several pages further in, another quadriplegic—
This one a few years older, thirty-one—
Has just requested permission from the state of Nevada
For euthanasia. He broke *his* neck diving in shallow water
While still a child; now, his father, his one caretaker,
Has been diagnosed with cancer.
As a young boy he believed the paralysis would be cured;
Once he knew he'd never get well, he decided on death—
Remaining fixed in conviction
For seventeen years. He lay on a gurney
And the world took its sweet time letting him lie there;
No one could help him and feel right about it;
No one knew if what he wanted was really the right thing;
No one was sure he was completely in his right mind,
And it wouldn't be fair to expect someone else
To go to prison for intervening in a case like that. . . .

All the stories we tell about ourselves end up
Apologetic. We want people to keep pretending we don't have it
So rough, we tone down the worst parts so no one is
Shocked, we offer anecdotes about *other* people—
Stories that make you feel bad because you already feel bad—
You talk about the boy diving into shallow water,
The newspapers taking his reckless exuberance
Which, except for a tragic circumstance, could not have been pointed to
As a flaw or failing
And making a solemn "example" of it—

Stories like this are sealing your fate;
You wonder how you will "take it" when tragedy befalls—
And you already know too much.
You know there's no way to know the thoughts in a human head,
Even when someone's been pared down so that's all that's left of him.
It came to you suddenly, like a name
You'd tasted on the tip of your tongue for days.
It was late, you were turning in,
Brushing your teeth, drying your face on a terry towel—
Suddenly, without emotion, you began to cry.
There was no other physical sensation, no feeling of exhaustion;
It was more as if you had come to know your life like your body
And there was no feeling in your body.
It was as if you had had no feeling for a number of years
But kept hoping for a cure.

The Innocent Embrace

After months of construction, the wide street opens,
No lines painted yet so each driver makes his way
Like a weed come up in a sidewalk crack.
Concrete dust dulls everything—the postered façade
Of the Pinewood Market (S.K. tuna 6 oz. can 65);
The dry red hair of a flea-ridden, three-legged hound;
A picture window behind which a Vietnamese boy tends
A cage of finches; a pregnant woman walking.
Her belly is boxy in a white shift; her legs could be
White paper, folding, unfolding.
She must not know, someone's wondering
How it feels to be full of an animal
Which, released, will howl, its face still moist
With membrane and mother's blood. She wouldn't say,
As someone's thinking, *the strident*
Sexplay of adolescence becomes unlucky
Parenthood, and nothing is understood. Walking,
Patiently, as if rocking a sick baby, the young woman
Turns her face to the cars passing in clouds
Of dust that draws the skin like alcohol, and the curious
Find her bland and fearless; and the one
Who wonders has driven on, blocks away by now, turning,
As she must, to herself, and the mist
Of all the years she hasn't lived yet,
And what will happen.

*

She was afraid of the dark. And there was room enough.
And it was innocent, the slim sickly only child
Held to the breast of the mother, the bedsprings
Groaning only a moment as the sleepers settled in.
The house was old and dreamed all night
Of prowlers in deep green overcoats, hand over hand up
The rose trellis bumping against the stucco;
In the girl's room a hundred plastic statuettes,
Collies and stallions rampant, kept watch
Over a cold bed dressed in pink chenille.
Each year, new excuses why she couldn't sleep

Alone: pneumonia, insects, a broken radiator,
Even the windows overlooking a big back yard
That cooed and squealed with screech owls,
Which, spot-lit, twisted cramped irascible faces
Toward the light, where suddenly hundreds of moths
Milled. The feathered bullet-bodies clamped on limbs
Were tiny and precise as nesting dolls
Or any toy made special for a delicate
And lonely daughter. In the manless house
Mother and child rattled like gravel, never touching
Except at night, within a cocoon of rose-print
And -scented sheets, dreaming of what it must be
To wake changed, winged, or never waking.

*

The house ticks itself to sleep, and takes him too,
But she's awake, thinking about the innocence of this
Embrace she's known from birth. She didn't sleep
Alone until her mother thought her old enough;
She was thirteen and getting breasts.
At thirty-five her breasts aren't that much bigger,
Unsuckled; she thinks they'll waste away.
The husband takes a long and noisy breath;
She pulls from under the arm that pulls her close.
Earlier, when they made love, she tried to think
Clinically—*the sperm is traveling to the egg.*
This time I'll conceive—though she'd taken a pill
That morning: the lie of purpose has become
A pleasure. She remembers pregnancy;
As if it were sickness, she was cured, and knew
Control, and felt her own familiar strength return
Like an old friend. But that was then. Tonight
She thinks of children, how they might sleep, having
Played hard, like puppies on the blond wood floor.
She thinks how she might pick them up and bring them
To her bed, one and one and one on the white spread,
And how she'd watch a dream come bubbling up
From sleep to a pale brow, and how she'd smooth it,
Her long fingers young again, her skin
Like theirs, clear and almost blue. She'd hold them

So, the way she knows can comfort and keep them
Whole. She'd hold them so they'd never grow.

While I'm Walking

Sometimes I like to tell people how they should live.
I think because I know a few secrets I have the answers
To everything, and that's not true. But sometimes the people
I speak to in my overbearing way listen, tilting
Their heads a little, implying they're not ready yet
To take my talk at face value. I might manage
To corner somebody most of an afternoon; one poor guy
Let his car idle while I crouched on my heels by his window.
I smiled in hard as I could and he didn't mind much,
But the tailpipe of his Toyota spat little puffs at the pavement,
In the parking lot outside the college where we both work,
In the iron gray parking lot under the slate gray sky
I claimed as the emblem of my empty life, the way I strain
To fill it with chatter, always saying something wrong.

When I find myself walking fast down brick sidewalks
And I can hear arguments drifting out windows,
Glass smashing, and the voices of both sexes raised in anger,
I stop listening to acorns crunching under my running shoes
And imagine bursting into the houses; and while I'm walking
My heart speeds up, and I keep walking. On these streets
The oaks are old enough to block the sky as well
As the roofs of the houses, and it's cooler in the shadow
Of the things people put there, and I wish those people had
Someone to talk to, I wish they could talk without arguing,
I wish somebody liked them so much, without going so far
As love, which they all secretly believe is out of reach.

Once I saw a man get mad because two people asked him
The same question. The second didn't even know of the first;
Anyone would've called the man unfair, unreasonable,
He stormed at the person who approached him
That unfortunate second time, and it was nothing,
Where's the restroom? or Where could I find a telephone?
He was a clerk, and the second person, a shopper, suggested
He "change his attitude" and made her way out of the store—
A department store, a small one, in a small town—
But though it ruined their day it improved mine, I could rest
Less alone in anger and wounded spirits. That was long ago,

So long it shouldn't matter; those years I just wanted
To buy new clothes and tease my hair and stay up late.
I had a reason for it, a good one, it was the only way
I could have the love I wanted, but it didn't work.

I know I'm going to look out one day and the sky will be
Changed so I'll know it's the end of the world. I mean
I'll know I've walked right to the end of it, where the sky
Hinges on, and for all the talks in darkened bars
And bedrooms, for all the waking trance of gazing
Into a thousand faces and loving one too many of them,
I will not even want to stop then. It might be the mistake
Of my life, following the sky, but sometimes I'm walking
And I see morning glories trained around a porch railing,
Sometimes I see lilies planted in a circle around a tree,
And I can't help watching their stems help them up,
Those soft stems stiffly furred and gently bending
So their blossoms arc the emblem of a journey—

I mean the journey to the sun. That's the one I'm on.
It's a long walk, and warm, and on the way I might have to
Take off my clothes and lie by the side. It's safe to do that
So far away and apart from everyone; I'm sure it's very safe.
Just like I'd be covered with such hard light
No one could see me, they'd turn their eyes away.

II

February

This is the second month of the year I turn thirty-seven.
Already the weather is warming in southeast Texas, rushing
The weeks along; the trees have to work to keep up. One day
I'll look over my head and the elm will be leafed out,
And then it will be summer. And probably I'll be working
On my birthday, probably teaching a couple of classes,
And I'll say to myself, it's just as well, who needs to think about
Turning thirty-seven, and I'll go back to my regular life,
Smiling and talking to students in the hallway,
Breaking a sweat on the short walk from the door
To the parked car, rolling all the windows down
But not without glancing at the sky for stormclouds,
Because a storm will be breaking every day then after noon,
Lasting about an hour, and subsiding back to sun. You learn
Such things about the weather when you've lived in a place
For a while. Or maybe it's really what some people say,
It's like that everywhere; I haven't been anywhere near
Everywhere, and maybe I'll never make it.
But there were years when I liked to search out danger,
Late nights I learned each secret worn-out cars
Bouncing through the ruts of logging roads could take me to.
I learned about love like that; the full moon pierced
The windshield like a spike and I knew it was love
When the strong, agile boy above me sighed
And pushed deeper inside me. I knew it was love
When I didn't want to close my eyes. I learned about trouble
And I knew it was trouble when I dropped out of high school
My senior year and took to prowling the roads with boys;
We took to shooting heroin under the spring sky,
We'd lie back together in the roadside grass and all let go
Of our suffering, we were having a hard time growing up,
It felt good to do a terrible thing together.
No one could find us there. No one was looking.
We would've counted the stars, but that was work.
Instead we talked about loving one another, and I guess
You'd say it was the heroin talking, but we thought we felt it,
We were free together, we knew how we were when no one
Could know us because we were doing evil. I took myself

Far from those foothills the first chance I could.
I didn't find out what became of my friends, it looked like
Some of them were headed for prison; I loved them once
But I wouldn't love them now, and I didn't want to
Think about mixing love and trouble, the trick I learned
And never gave up; I just got older, and stopped
Getting into the trouble of the young. I discovered
The troubles of the older.
                                    This is the second month
Of the year I turn thirty-seven. Already the little fists
Of leaves are forming inside the knotted ends of twigs
All over Houston. The cold weather is over. This winter
Again there was no freeze. And tonight it's very late,
And it's Sunday, and no cars pass on the big road
By the house, but out there in the night
Some kids about seventeen are doing terrible things
They'll get by with, and grow out of, and remember
The way they'll remember what love felt like at first,
Before it stopped being the surest path to ruination,
Before it had done the worst it could and passed away.
And to them it's as if those who lived this life before them
Moved with the jerky speeded-up gestures of characters
In old-fashioned movies, their expressions intense
And exaggerated; they roll their eyes and loll their tongues
When the heroin hits their blood. It's as if the beauty
Of evil lives only in the present, where the drop of dope
Clinging to the tip of the stainless steel point
Catches the light like dew; and it doesn't matter
That the light falls from a streetlamp with a short in it,
And the impatient boy with the syringe in his hand
Will touch the drop back into the spoon
So as not to waste it. It's his instinct telling him
How much it means to live this now, before he knows
Better, while he still has a chance to survive it.
It's the moon over his head with its polished horns
That would slip through his skin if he touched them.
It's the trees leaping to life in his blood, greenness
Unfurling so hard it almost bursts his heart.

The Mirror

Twee's Texaco, Elliston, Virginia, 1970

His face inches from the damp glass,
He repeats one word to his reflection;
And he is masturbating. Having stumbled on him,
I am not sure how to back away. If he looked
He'd see me in the mirror, one of the fragile
Spiders called *grandfathers* dangling near my face
From a wrecked web. Beyond the fog of breath on the glass,
The block walls white-washed high as an arm's reach,
The world I have just forgotten is filthy rich
With spring, and incorruptible; and I am young
And always going wrong and untouched, intractable.
Maybe the world has had enough of my girlishness
And has led me by my puffy sleeve into the men's
Restroom; it will always lead me where I have not been:
There is a question to draw me on, an answer
To stop me cold, the male voice with a sob in it,
And the rhythmic word *worthless worthless worthless*—
And the sweat forming at lip and temple,
The dry contractions of the pelvis, the friction
Of skin just audible; and a sore love for the past,
Which sickens, which he could not tell me
Even if I married him fresh from his own hands
And nurtured him as he might require, even if
I dared to speak or lay a hand cold with compassion
To slow the arm, facile, tender, to forestall. . . .
I am still new at this. And so quiet, I can watch
For a while without his knowing, as I must.
And he knowing more than I would even believe.

Genesis

"Joys impregnate. Sorrows bring forth."
—Proverbs of Hell

She would have had me believe that I, not yet existing,
Was nevertheless of strong enough will to bring together
Consenting adults in an act that should never have happened,
They didn't want it but had no choice, forced into coitus
By a drive not their own so I might be conceived,
And my father, not cursed with the burden of bearing me,
Could then escape into the gray nowhere to live the rest of his youth
Forgetting the night in the motel room my mother knew
From her job on the road, the bedevilment of my incipient will
Screwing their pelvises together in what must have been
Painful, embarrassing, even as it took place.
She would have had me imagine him rising onto his elbows
To try to pull away, their eyes meeting in unspeakable shame
Because she was decent and middle-aged, almost into menopause,
He ambitious and nineteen, destined for more chaste success,
And finding himself locked and helpless, thrusting
As if some unseen machine had him by the hips.
I used to pity her to the point of tears whenever I asked about
My father and her face moved like a ghost had a hold on it,
Her voice got smaller to fit her throat like his cock
Nailed her for no better purpose than to beget a daughter
Like me, whose tears at being left with my grandmother
Every Sunday for thirteen years while Mother went on the road
Were not nearly payment for what *I* had done,
Breaking into life like a bank and stealing all the money.
She taught me sex was *supposed* to hurt girls as greedy
As me, girls like me could rest assured we'd find plenty
Of men to leave us, we'd pin them too long
Between our legs and they'd burst up, coughing,
Secretly pleased to have "gotten what they wanted."
I never admitted a word of it even as it came true,
Even after she quit her job and married and moved away
And whatever I felt turned into the highway
I drove fourteen nights without stopping at one
Of the sleazy motels stretching pale pink feet in the road;
I wasn't out of high school yet, or it wasn't time to be.

It served me right to land in jail for using Mother's credit card
To sleep in the Atlanta Hilton; she went through my pockets
While cops held my arms till her hand closed on plastic.

Sometimes when I make love the thing it feels most like
Is hate. It's not the vision of Mother and Father
Grinding away in the vise I created; it's not the men
Who wondered why I always questioned everything
And fucked me because of it. It's not even
My taciturn husband, who's had the chance
To hate me himself; it's me, in all my bewildering
And harsh intensity, cutting myself from the whole cloth
Of the innocent nineteen-fifties, crushing the life
From my own parents before they could even anticipate me;
Fulfilling the worst prophecies with a sense of manifest destiny;
Letting a pack of crazy lies move into my big skull: I hate myself
For ever believing I rocked my own cradle into being,
For the anger and strength and persistence
I suffer myself to bear into the world.

Bridget

As I remember, I was that kind of girl. I was
Like Bridget, I read about her in the Plain Dealer,
Who was shot in the arm because her brother wanted
To live with his mother. "We'll kill ourselves if we don't
Get to," they dared the SWAT team, and the team killed
Their friend Jason. The entire telephone transcript
Started on the front page, it was lengthy, many shots
Were fired, and Jason died for the sake of strength,
He found out he had none, he flew into a rage
Because a cop tossed a pack of cigarettes, bought
To calm him, onto the deck instead of into his hand;
He fired at the cop, he missed, no cops were killed.
Then they blasted a hole in his neck. That was
The way Bridget described it, sobbing into the phone,
"My friend has a hole in his neck." Her brother said,
"My partner has a gap in his mouth." Bridget said,
"There's blood sticking out." She's fourteen.
She was shot in the arm. She was standing behind Jason.
She told the police she had to be there for her brother
Wanting to live with their mother. I was like that.
I got in trouble because of boys. I tagged along
When they committed crimes, I held their dope, they said
There was no way I'd be searched but it wasn't true,
The cops were smarter and the cops were mean,
They figured out a way. The cops told Jason
He wasn't in trouble so he wouldn't shoot himself.
He called them fuckers. They told Brian he wasn't
In trouble, then arrested him. That's what Jason said
They'd do, for once he was right. It's not the law
Not to lie to kids. There are good reasons to lie
To kids, if they're hurting themselves, or they might
Hurt others; that's what cops say. Maybe they're right.
But cops made me take off my clothes for them;
And they were in uniform.

I was like Bridget. I wanted to do right by boys.
Sometimes they'd smile in my direction, showing
Bad teeth that proved they were country; sometimes

They promised they'd take care of me. I don't know
What happened the night I went to jail. I stared down
The angles of the blue-strobed field, we'd had a wreck
By a pasture, there were cops, there were parents,
I mean my mother and stepfather, it was a small town,
A southern small town, and I went to jail at seventeen
To keep the boys from going. Bridget was shot.
She'll never recover. I never did. I feel like you,
Bridget, but now I know better, I wish you did;
I like to say I never knew my father. You must've
Been living with yours. I know how it feels
To take too long to figure it out: they don't want us,
Bridget, we're a fuck to them, that's how we got here
And how they'd touch us if the law allowed; it does,
They fucked us good. Nothing makes us feel
Ourselves like a fuck we've felt before, if it's father,
A cold hard fuck, if it's mother, a wet sloppy fuck,
If it's brother, short and quick like a ferret's tongue,
Like the feet of the hamster racing his wheel
Every night while we dream of men; if we wake up
We'll begin to fear them. Now in my dream I hear
The voice of your brother calling 911, I dream
The shapes of his features screwed up as he cries,
"The cops just shot my partner," and "Somebody come
Please help my partner," and his partner was dead.
I dream the question of the sides of the law.
Bridget, we have to hide ourselves, because we can't
Help it, we want to help, and it always seems right,
There are men on each side, sometimes they extend
A hand that looks able to hold much more than ours,
Their voices are saying, "Come to me, come, only
Here I'll protect you," and you don't say no
To a smile like that. You rush to kneel by the fallen
Friend, wet teeth shining through a gap in his head.

The Accident

I had no business there in the first place—
I'm putting on weight—but the counter help was all smiles,
Having survived the lunch hour crunch. My husband and I
Ordered burgers and fries; I was in front, so I chose
A seat on the far side, back to the window.
I picked off two thin rings of onion; the fries were limp.
We were talking about some recent trouble,
Something about the car, maybe, both of us
Interested, me a little bitchy, so it was almost the way you turn
Instinctively, say from a spider web in a darkened hall,
How I looked across the restaurant and found her face,
Left cheekbone swollen to a baseball, the same eye blackened,
Heavy make-up, front tooth out in a jack-o-lantern grin
As she tried to look friendly to the young waitress
Her husband motioned over. He rested one hand
On his wife's shoulder, solicitous, the other waving
A lit cigarette, a small man, dark-haired, now laughing aloud,
Glancing at the uncombed head of his beaten wife again
Turning her back to the room, though not crowded,
All suddenly staring, reading the last few hours
Of those lives in a horror of recognition.
She cupped her hand shading the side of her face,
You could see lumps of vertebrae through her t-shirt,
And he kept on talking, smiling at her, with a slight tilt
Of his head, as if saying *poor baby, something happened to her,*
Good thing I'm here to take care of her, a car wreck,
A bad one, a smash-up, and all of us looked
And knew better. At the table with them was a little girl.
The man, the woman, the five-year-old daughter—
Even the man and the beaten woman had the same features,
As people do who have lived together for years. I couldn't see
The child's face. He was jotting a note on a small pad,
The waitress's name, as if to write a letter praising
Her fine service, and she smiled through her horror, she
Hardly more than sixteen, with clear pale skin. Next to us
A woman in permed hair and suit rose to leave, lunch untouched,
With her daughter. She carried a leather legal-size folder.
We left soon after, heads turned, not looking,

Because sometime the man and woman would go
Home to the privacy of a city apartment, no neighbors
Home all day to hear, but first I said, in the restaurant,
Across the room where he couldn't hear, *If I had a gun*
I'd blow his brains out, and I thought of that moment
Familiar from movies, the round black hole in the forehead
Opening, the back of the skull blowing out frame by frame
Like a baseball smashing a window, but no one near
Would've even been bloodied because no one was standing anywhere
Near him, his hand on the beaten woman's shoulder
Might as well've been yards from his body.

I was taught not to write about this. But my teacher,
A man with a reputation who hoped I would make
Good, never knew that I, too, have been hit in the face by a man.
He knew only my clumsy efforts to cast what happened
Into "characters," and he loved beauty in poetry.
Maybe what I had written was awkward. Maybe my teacher
Guessed what happened and forbade me writing it
For some good reason, he cared for me, or he feared
He too might've slapped my face, because I, like the character
In that first effort, was bitching to the heavens and a redneck
Boyfriend, and we argued outdoors, near a stack of light wood
Used to kindle the stove like everyone has
In the foothills of North Carolina. That day I railed
Like a caricature of a bitching redneck woman,
Hands on hips, sometimes a clenched fist, I was
Bitching, I think, as he planned some stupid thing
I hated, like fishing, pitching horseshoes, driving
To visit his mother on Sundays, her tiny house
Tangled in dirt roads, where she sat in the kitchen dipping snuff.
Whatever he wanted to do was harmless,
But so was my shrieking, my furious pleading, an endless loop
Inside my head rolling *I want to be rid of him*, and he slapped me
Across my open mouth, I felt myself shut up and staggered,
Because he was a large man, and I was a large woman,
He had to make sure he hit me pretty hard,
Both of us strong and mad as hell, early
One Saturday morning, when he wanted to do what he wanted to do
And I wanted to keep him from it. He slapped me
Twice, open-handed, knocking me, open-handed, to my knees
In kindling, so my knees were scraped bloody and my hand
Closed on a foot and a half of inch-thick pine, and I stumbled up,

Swinging, my eyes popping wide, till I brought it down
Hard across his shoulder, I saw how the rage on his face
Flashed to fear, just that quick, a second, or less,
And he turned to run but he made the wrong choice,
If he'd gone to the road I wouldn't've followed, but he ran
Inside my "duplex" apartment, an old country house
Cut in two. So I cornered him upstairs and knocked him out.
It was simple. He fell so hard, I thought *I've killed him;*
I was throwing my clothes in a paper bag when I heard him
Sobbing. In the bathroom mirror I found the black eye and lop-sided lip,
And it seemed as if I might still take it back, the last ten minutes,
The chase, the beating, the high-pitched screaming,
The stubborn need to go fishing. But the make-up I disdained
In those years—I had just turned twenty—didn't do much
To cover the bruises. His face was clear. The knot on his head
Stopped swelling under ice. It was easy to tell him
To get the hell out and only regret it every other minute
Since there were no children, no marriage, even,
And I was young and believed I had proven
I was strong. I had beaten a man to his knees.
Months later I would go to college and stay safely there for years,
Not letting on to anyone the terrible thing I'd done, until I wrote
That clumsy poem with the unbelievable characters, and now I've tried
To do it again, this time with different characters, I've defied
My teacher, who meant for me to learn to write well,
Who meant for the world to think well of me,
And I am not sorry. If he asked why I would say
I had to do it, and that lie would be like the lie of living
Without telling, till one day seeing the beaten face,
What scared me most, the missing tooth, the tangled hair, the vertebrae,
The daughter. There is no use thinking what it means
About me to say this: I am not sorry. I might have killed
That man. I might have blown his brains out.

III

The Heart And The Symbol

We traverse impatiently the landscape of dislike,
Which is not a winter landscape, or yet a desert;
There is not the beauty of pronged saguaro
To sustain hope's last shred. Nothing requires
Adaptation. It is too well known, we could find our way
Drunk with the lights out, as on the curvy road
Where our houses are the last houses and have been
Always. And because each leathery dead leaf
Curling its edges like an old photograph
Is familiar as the taste in our mouths each morning,
We find this landscape not without comfort.
The body-armored police sergeant directing traffic,
His eye fixed on the driver's eye as a factory worker
Might match razor-sharp metal plates for size,
One disc to the other—what's certain about him
Is the way he's caused trouble, his vast potential
For more; there's no doubt what he thinks about
The young woman who swerves too close
On purpose. Whenever we meet our rivals
Unexpectedly, we are apt to shake hands, brush
Faces smooth as polished bone. Clasping shoulders
We can just make out faded slogans on billboards
Blocks away, like the distant, derided memory
Of how we felt before refinement took over
Our souls, teaching us the smile behind the sword.
The truth is, we'd reach into the other's body
And disentangle each clumsy organ,
Its twin still pulsing beneath our own skins.
Like an opal that loses its fire when taken from water
And worn dry for a while, the stone in the kidney;
Like meat set before the laborer, whose hunger
Drives guilt and the meal of thought
Down through his guts undigested, the one idea
Remaining that *now he will keep working;*
Like the red oak dead seven seasons ago, some months
Indistinguishable from the living oak beside—
The beauty of the landscape is the beauty
Of structure, never producing out of itself

But standing under and within, the very shape
Of our lives, which does not bend and is slow to break—
So we believe. There is something inside us too,
We can feel it, it is the stick figure we drew
As children, even then outlined without a heart
Or the need for one, but fully clothed, in triangular
Skirts or transparent trousers, the stalk of leg
Inside neatly irrelevant beside the house, its gabled roof,
The sun beating down dots and dashes.

Revisions

One sponge of Spanish moss droops, dabbing
The classroom window. And the turn of pages,
The erasures, are sponges squeezed
Into scrub-buckets, so teacher will never know.
But she will notice the paper roughened,
A word revised, a phrase, and think
He was probably right the first time.
No one will ever know, least of all the young man
Who writes with his nose an inch from the paper,
Fast, the better to forget. *He is so right,*
She thinks, *to get rid of words, if only*
Because they can *be changed, and lost—*

Sometimes she and a man go to movies,
For darkness and the big screen; once,
After a film beleagured with symbols
Of fecundity, they talked of the large genitals
Of farm animals, of humans, mammals,
Having nothing to do but fuck, relentless,
Dutiful, probably not even knowing why,
The mare standing hobbled to be mounted,
The pornographic movie star trying to keep it up
Under lights, the camera's whirr like a rattlesnake—
He told her. She has not forgotten.
She has taken to loving the talk
He loves, of anger, of childhood, of having
To find, firsthand, irrevocable
Proof that nothing can be said well.
In bed she talks, and is angry, and becomes
Childlike, with a need to know, and the lover
Grows hard and harder, and mistakes
Are rubbed, as with pumice, rubbed out—

As under friction a desktop squeals, some thought
Worn through; next the chirrup of a pencil-point
Loading the emptied line with words, like a rat
Lining its nest with paper and bits of moss.
It has been done over so many times, all wrong

If teacher saw, who likes the class to pretend
To believe the crisp infallibility
Of her critical eye. Often, their attention
Wanders; it seems to her they dream of sex.
They are weak with naïve sleep and desire;
Relaxed, their legs fall open. To her
It's like hearing a baby cry
And imagining its face at her breast,
Though she has borne no children.

True Confessions

You know how easy it is to let an idea take hold of you.
You feel yourself changing the way you feel a horse set off trotting;
You close your legs. At least that's how it works with me.
Somehow I got it into my head, men would love me for my body.

It was just as well to think such a thing. I was seventeen and determined
Not to let a chance go to waste. The world rolled out its lucky
Breaks, and though now there is, to my mind at least,
Something suspect about making these admissions,

I was able to enjoy sex with many men before, or even
At the moment as, I understood myself to have—to them—no meaning.
As I interpreted my own thinking, even as a girl, "meaning"
Was incipient, dependent on things apart from sexuality;

It remained incipient for some time. I seem to remember
Consciously thinking, the only way to make up what I lacked
Was to "run through" men. I wanted—needed—to learn them
Like phone numbers. My subtlest taste would be slight

Differences. Oh, I could feel it the minute he set foot
On the stairs to my trailer; and I could tell which one
He was, too, without looking, even before he said hello
And the dog either barked or knocked over the magazine rack,

Wagging his tail. I worked in a factory then
Like all the town girls, selling Avon at break, getting in trouble for it,
Sanding bed frames and dreaming about screwing,
Because in there you couldn't talk. The fans made too much noise.

Everywhere you read it says teenage boys think of sex all day.
As a teenager I thought of sex all day and watched
Teenage boys and thought of how they think of sex all day,
And I thought they were thinking of sex then, and I tried hard

To tell by looking at them what kind of sex they thought of.
I often thought about my body and wondered when, if ever, men
Thought of it. I was conscious of my arms pressing my breasts together
When I reached out to steady the piece I was sanding.

I was young and wanted sex all the time. I never got pregnant
But had trouble other ways, nabbed by parents,
Police, park rangers, razzed by friends, fucked over by jerks in love
With me for a few minutes. I was "intense," "great

In bed," a walking anvil of rage, a complete phony. I fell in love
So easily. It felt good every time. I thought it was fine
For love to start at the center of the body and penetrate outward,
As if love were a flowering pea vine and the pea must be pressed in

Where the soil takes water. I thought—and for a while
Circumstances proved me right—that the course of my life
Would tend toward passion, an active
Participation in sexual love finally revealing to me

The infinite possibilities of my libidinistic urges
As worked upon by others' urges—usually more experienced, at least
More orchestrated. I still feel it to talk about it—magnificent
Sensitivity! But I was a better critic than artist.

You see how it moves me even today, the memory of coming of age,
Of the young men's bodies surprising me with their strength,
Of their excitement when they moved to touch me,
Of my own boldness and expertise outstripping my excitement.

That was my dream at seventeen, and it was, after its fashion,
Fulfilled. I have lived half a life under the shadow of sex.
I have, today, a *jaded* taste. . . . I suppose I exaggerate.
But what do you do for someone who's had everything—

Or everyone—and outlived it into matrimony? When the body—
Not the only thing, but once loved for what it can be no longer—
Resists with obvious neutrality? And when the heart
Still stammers, embarrassing youth, *it doesn't know?*

Red Ribbon

Route 11, north of Bristol, Virginia; a house
trailer, two-tone, turquoise and white

The city limits range like livestock
Into the stands of pine hackling hillsides;
Just within them a sign ringed in flashing lights
Makes a pale spot in the night, like bleach
Splashed on workpants. The name spelled
In neon letters reads "The Red Ribbon";
The clientele comes from the coal mines,
Or they're salesmen, having taken one look, relieved
To be leaving in the morning. The young women
Like it that way, ducking out of College Algebra,
In their backpacks garter belts and back-seamed
"Black Diamond" stockings, push-up bras
In slither-red satin, spike heels, and corselets.
They work for tips, and will take MasterCard;
Slow afternoons, they sit together, used to
One another's undress, and discuss love,
Which they believe in. One of the girls
Loves a customer; thick-bodied, bellicose,
Moist, dark, and married, he drops in
Every Wednesday and asks for her.
He's even asked to take her out, "where fucking's free,"
She says, but she likes it better at the Red Ribbon,
Where she knows to the nickel what she's worth,
And nothing else.

*

A tall boy with hips requests a modeling session.
A twenty-dollar camera's unlocked from a bottom drawer;
He has to be shown the shutter button.
In the dull brown, close, trailer bedroom,
A nude woman poses like a pin-up,
Knees pressed together, lips pursed;
The young gentleman takes polaroids
And lines them up on the dresser top to develop.
That's all he wants—behind a black box,
To let the glass eye look first.

In the flashbulb's burst their faces are lost,
Except for hers, on film; as if they knew one another
Too well, they find the blindness exciting.
Only the light makes love, unwatched,
And there's no talk. He takes another twenty
From his wallet; she opens her legs to the light.
A hairnet of perspiration falls across her face,
But even in the last shot she looks straight
Into the lens, clear, persistent, still untouched,
As if she could see through the cloud floating,
Purple velvet, in every direction;
As if she could look past the black box
The boy holds like a mask, and see through distance,
Desire, ground glass, fear, the profound
And soothing harmlessness.

                        *

Say you're driving a loaded truck down the mountain,
About to the bottom and damn glad to let off
The smoking brakes and shake the hairpin turns
Like hairpins holding you in place.
Say it's November, and the earth is dappled,
Punk wood, fungus, a hundred summers'
Leaves, mahogany and mushroom-colored.
A two-lane ropes the knob; water runs the culverts
From the night's rain, bubbling, stumbling
On sandstone and clay, taking bits of it,
Invisible, along. Among the jumble of rounded peaks,
Cabins and shacks make sense; you think
What it took to put them up, hewing lumber
On the site so the same pine stands, not much
Changed, a talisman. But on the north slope
You spot a mobile home, burned long ago
So the oak limbs overhanging are healed.
Now you're driving faster than ever,
Hurtling downhill while the trailer seems to rise,
Blackened, indestructible, as if from earth.
The heater's on full blast; the engine knocks
As you try to catch up to the trailer floating
Through fall's true sienna; you think
You've been driving like this for days,
Pursuant, enraptured, puzzled at the impossible
Placement of something so ugly it must be man's,
So far gone it could be a god's.

The Visitor

He was saying he might come back that night.
Truck idling, road-dusty, door open—
He claimed his car wouldn't crank, blown starter—
He wasn't trying to look too friendly;
She was watching his arm, the splotch of tattoo,
Hands etched with sun, the blunt fingers.
He works construction, hangs out in town;
Though she likes it he's not like the others,
The farmers, always talking soybean, melon,
Summers, it's true their backs' labor, dumb
And field-strong, brings forth vine and stalk.

He said he might come back, but at midnight
She swallows a valium, gives him up.
Almost—closing the bedroom window on
Spears of corn, brandished in the scant light
Of a slivered crescent moon, she hardly feels
The tranquilizer, except that an hour ago
Her nerves were shot, and now she's just wound
A little tight but normal, she thinks, wanting
The crunch of tires on gravel, then a scent
Like metal—that would be his body.
She would love the surprise of his body.

Do stars hiss in the damp hands of a cloud?
She sleeps deeply and doesn't see, no lights
Brighten the two-lane. No truck tires crunch.
So when she burrows into body-warmth,
She doesn't open her eyes at first.
She dreams it's better, arms pinning her
In darkness: velvet under winter sky—
She dreams arithmetic, six discrete arms
Of a snowflake. Then, he's erect. Then, inside,
Dry. She doesn't know him. She's not sure.
Before she can tell him to stop, he stops.

It's late. One pale green blur of alarm clock hands
Lies face down telling the floor so. The August
Wind, having flown all night, crawls slack-jawed

On thin bare knees; the moon drops below a blank
Horizon; somebody's crazy rooster crows,
But it's too late for light. It's not early.
Then somebody says so. His voice is not
His voice. *It's late.* Waiting for his weight to lift,
She feels semen leak out, and thinks, *it's late.*
His face is darkness. So are his shoulders.
That's why her muscles, falling asleep, shudder.

The visitor, she calls him. But she is here
To stay. She's learned his name, and where he lives,
One of those farms full of shit-kicking farm boys
Who know how to act like they're happy as hell
Picking suckers off tobacco, four months
Out of the year: she'd caught him stumbling
Drunk through cornstalks folding around him
Like bad water; nude from the waist down, nothing
But ugly, he sobbed *I'm lost.* She believed him.
That night she was sure she'd just forget him.
Still, her shame wavers, the flame of a candle.

She wonders what to call what happened.

Responsibility

It did no good to think, or to stop thinking. It did no good
To think in a straight line, or a starburst, or a circle.
It did no good to think driving down the highway,
Or walking alone in a park with live alligators.
It was no use thinking what had happened, or what
Was going to happen. If there'd been one image
She could've dreamed to make the thoughts move over,
She would've bowed to its significance: a fallen-down barn
Against empty sky. Sidewalks strewn with clippings
In a suburban neighborhood where the residents walk
After the sun goes down. The silhouette of a man
Straightening his tie. But no image would shake into focus;
Each swam into the next. It did no good to speak,
Or to stop speaking. It did no good to look, or to stop looking.
Her eyes closed when she felt sleepy, and when she woke
Nothing was different. Her eyes opened when light
Shone through the window; the light was different
From the light that stayed on in the hall at night,
But nothing else was different. If the air was cool,
That was the extent of it. If the air was close and warm,
That was the extent of it. She looked at her feet that paced
The wood floor for hours, getting nowhere. She looked
At the shape of her calves, thinner, harder, from walking.
She looked at her knees, disappointing knees under
A layer of skin that just got thicker. She saw she had
The legs of an animal; she saw she had the hands
Of an animal. She looked in the mirror and saw she had
The snout of an animal, two holes to breathe through.
That was something to think about; but the trouble
With thinking was it didn't go anywhere, there was
A shape inside her head like a loaf of bread,
Pressing so things went blurry. Then she thought
It must be time she was looking at, that's why
She couldn't see at a distance; she took out her pencil
And made a list of questions. Her animal hand
Scratched marks on paper her animal eyes couldn't read.
Her animal eyes closed in the darkness, she had worked
Very hard without thinking about it, and nothing

Was different. There was nothing to do but wait
For time to catch up. It was going to be a long wait,
What with the moon passing through its phases,
People dying without saying goodbye, decisions made
Without asking permission, and the body still
Just the shell that keeps something alive inside.
If she hadn't waited so long already, she might've learned
To stop thinking about it, but she was in a hurry,
And in that way stopped herself as no one else could,
No one else holding, as she did, the hands of time.
It was as if she'd offered to sit by the sickbed of a loved one,
But the illness was long and debilitating, and the mind
Went first; and when the patient died, she wasn't free
To go, but had to remain by the decomposing body.
It was just an idea she had, to sit by the body; but no one
Was there to release her from her duty, and no one
Could've convinced her that wasn't her proper place.

IV

Red Tulips

Next you'll be saying it doesn't matter
If a woman never knows happiness.
You'll be saying it bitterly because if
I listen it will mean I have one more
Reason to stop thinking about what
Will happen, and you're not sure you
Want that on your conscience.
I have an idea about your conscience.
I imagine you rummaging through it
Sunday afternoons, dressed in sweats
And no makeup. The red tulips
You paid the gardener extra to plant
Bloom behind your back in a riot,
Like children mocking adult
Proprieties, but you can ignore that.
You know without looking how
Their barrel heads splay to reveal
Stamens like carpet tacks; it's no
Secret how spring wears itself out.
You're looking for a photograph,
You and your young husband; you said
He looked so handsome. For once
I kept my mouth shut, having respect
For the living, if not the dead. But he
Was no more handsome than the men
I've loved, and they weren't handsome
Beyond my eyes taking them in.

You said I'd better watch out. I can't
Take care of myself. Women who don't
Know how to stay married end up
In trouble. They end up carrying
Their possessions with them everywhere,
Wearing all their clothes at once,
And secreted in the clothing is a photo.
They might have to take off two sweaters
Just to get at it, but to them the photo
Is worth the work. It is a man who was

Beautiful in their eyes. It is a photo
That should be painful to look at,
But at long last there is no pain left.
You said numbness is the blessing
Of hell, which saves us dying
The good death, chosen the moment
We see the last of love. You said I have to
Think about living a long time because
Women outlive their husbands.
They have to live a long time alone.

I haven't told you about the photo of red
Tulips. I could show it to you this minute,
But I don't want to look at it again.
To me red tulips mean the end of love.
I remember noticing the petals had fallen
From their stalks one day I carried away
My belongings, so when I saw red tulips
Laughing behind your back, I could
Hardly be surprised. Their cruelty
Is too familiar. They bloom even when
You cry hard inside the house;
But if you look to them for comfort,
A reminder of the heart's strong color,
On that day to be famous for endings,
They will have shed their satin. But
They don't mind holding up their naked
Stalks; they won't be shamed.

Friends are no help to one another.
They give advice and want it taken.
They talk to each other like turning
To the east at dawn, to pray, to see the sun
Rise, to keep up the habit of turning.
They feel too deeply the other's wrongs,
They would prevent them if they could.
I know you would give me a husband
Like yours, but I wouldn't love him.
In the photo he's blond as a barn cat,
Tall and lean, and it used to be you
Next to him, but you tore yourself away
When you had the gift of prophecy.
It had it too, once; I stained the knees

Of a new pair of jeans kneeling to snap
That shot of tulips splayed and glossy
Under the late spring sun. I was sure
I would never see them again. It was
The last season for blossoms like that,
That shade of red like satin ribbon.

Criticism

Everyone agreed, that scene is the most moving
Where the character played by the lead actress
Not so much *reveals* her tragic past and long-lingering grief,
As *recognizes* sorrow in another woman and feels for *her;*
When the stern expression we have come to accept
In an hour and a quarter as, irrevocably, Ida's,
Undergoes the miraculous, gentle transformation
From the utile brittle and zipped civil to anger on behalf
Of another; when she cries "I *hate* your father!"
And the director does us the rare favor of allowing
The obvious paternal connection to make *itself*—
No whisking through time to muttonchops, bottles
Of bey rum, an "exquisite" miniature portrait—
We suck in our breath as one, the audience,
An intricate understanding of a familiar circumstance
Unfolding inside us like a multicolored fan,
Several tiers and elaborate central structure,
Understanding to stuff every one of us,
No matter how huge our empty spaces; still leaving
A sense of anticipation, because surely what we learn next,
Both at the moment we watch the action and later
The time we talk about it, will be the pithy, exact
Heart of compassion, where it grows like a vine
Surprisingly coarse and hard to uproot;
How it got there, like seeds caught in the feathers
Of a dark, frightening bird and scattered far
From their source; and whoever relates the story
Will find himself clipping each word with a strong
Inflection, to keep from blurting out everything;
And though he has watched with sympathy
Whatever *he* could reveal; though if the woman
Blocking part of his view with her lacquered hair
Like a coxcomb had turned to observe him
At the height of emotion he shared with the giants
On the screen, the sharing would have been
Clear enough indeed; a feeling he would refer to
Inaccurately as "instinct" correctly advises him,
He would tell all, every moment of it,
And none of it anyone's business but his own.

Eclipse

On codeine—another botched root canal—
I missed most of the lunar eclipse;
Trying to keep my eyes open, I stared
At a lousy movie I'd rented, *Shakedown*,
About crack, crooked cops, clichéd blacks.
A huge polished credenza fairly groaned
Under stacks of c-notes; this was life
As nobody knows it, all the coke dealers
Enormous bucks, limousined and braceleted,
Their peach-shaped heads clean-shaven. Oh, white men
Came off greedy, too, yet on the side
Of the law; women trembled, addicted
To the acrid smoke they spent their paychecks
And, finally, their sex for. But let me
Rewind the evening a moment: earlier,
In "Whole Foods," I'd bought organic apples
And boysenberries the size of a thumb joint
For my pet birds. The slightest mist
Of pesticide might kill them: my nightmare,
Interrupted sleep when neither codeine
Nor antihistamine gives my waking
Consciousness an alibi for restraint,
Returns like a miser to his cache
Of bankbooks, plays slow-mo a grainy film
Of cockatiels pinioned in plastic boxes,
Their wings' harps yellow as filtered moonlight,
Discolored with dark blood. But the beaming
Woman at the register in the overpriced
Health food store told me about the lunar
Eclipse, that minute becoming visible above
The tattered canopy of the out-of-business
Seafood shop next door. Sure enough,
The whole moon, big-city stained, had a bite
Out of its left side, leaving me hungry
For more. My molar, reamed twice in the space
Of a week of living nerve and pulp, ached
Like something alien had grown there;
Halfway through *Shakedown* the thrice "recommended
Dosage" codeine it took to absolve me

Of mortal pain chopped the end of the plot:
This much I know, there was gunplay. A blonde's
Body slumped forward, over a velvet chair.
Then it was the house next door—live soundtrack,
I mean, my neighbor, Dan, shouting, the crunch
Of a beercan between his hand and the hood
Of his Chevrolet: I *saw* that part,
Stumbling to the window like someone wounded,
Parting the blinds for eyeshot. But here was more
Soliloquy than shadowplay: it seemed
He'd fallen in love with the moon, or
Hated the earth's shape roughly projected
Like the image on a drive-in screen, now
Exiting stage right, silent as a mime.
He raised his arms—he would take her
In them, he vowed, and he was ready:
You bitch, he was screaming, *come down here,*
I've got a hardon, you're chickenshit,
If you're going to give it to me ever,
Baby, hurry up and get it over with.
My role in this was limited: I'd sneaked
Into the theater, catching clips from the previews.
But it wasn't just fear he'd turn his desire
On someone more accessible than untouchable
Artemis making me wish he had something
To hurt and love at once besides himself,
Even the flimsy web-seat lawn chair
He finally pitched at his roof, missed, and dodged
Its clumsy tumble back to gravity.
What is there in the world to love like that?—
Nothing like the two dalmatians he claimed
Were stolen by his former wife: he'd kept them
Chained to howl by his door; not his ex-wife,
Who must've decided she'd snatch
What she wanted of love from a tether: I mean,
If he's right, she preferred his hounds to him.
It would take a goddess or a dark round shadow
Cast by something inert as a planet
To absorb what he felt without turning it
Back with force enough to kill a man—
Especially him, in his aviator glasses
Out of joint at the temple, his habit
Of pissing on the side of his house

The gallons of "lite" coursing through him
Like a bayou. He's threatened to shoot *my* dog,
And to show me he would he shot my house,
Excising the eye of William Blake from the stacks
Of books by the sofa. But last night
Even the moon left him, the huge dark shadow
Of earth; I knew then if I had the money
I'd rent a new place tomorrow. Yet
When I leaned there, loaded on codeine,
The phantom pain of my empty tooth
Like a slug fired into my jaw, the red light
Of the VCR all that was left of the flick
About dope other dope had saved me
Seeing through, I wouldn't've minded shooting
The moon, the fake danger of swearing in half-
Light, the reaching up, falling back to earth
And the flat plastic arms of a sun-rotted
Lawn chair: *Come down here, cocksucker.*
Why don't you hurry up! I could beat
The hell out of you, I could love you,
I could, I could prove it.

The Unbeliever

Well, spring comes early here. So much the better
For those dull humans who react like bears
To winter. Sorrow, sleep, no appetite —
I know the symptoms. Suffering from lack
Of sun corrupts the sense of holidays
My relatives can celebrate without
Irony, sardonic comments on God's willingness
To shore up weak economies, and pained
Expressions at all toasts to good fortune.
My atheism, December-blooming rose,
Allows no such paroxysms of "false faith."
The sky is dark; where could this God be hiding?
Thus in childhood my sole religious pleasure
Occurred, recurred, among the lit tapers
Of Christmas Eve, for here I found some proof
Of Holy Spirit: every candle bore
The same flame, as one fire in splinters; each
Late arrival to the midnight service,
The breeze that passed through pews when heavy doors
Opened and closed, awoke in hundreds of
Tiny fires the same impulse — bend away,
As leaves curve from blown twigs, in concert, all
Anchored alike. But outside, elms, white oaks,
Maples, had long since given up on light
And, like me, dropped their leaves. We shared one view
Of winter; it was time to stand ashamed
And naked, they of greenness, I of joy.
My saving grace was human. I could move
Where little lights reminded me of summer,
The soul of summer, anyway, but trees
Were rooted to their cyclical penance.
I would have wept for them but used my tears
To stand for my own grief instead. At ten
I didn't call it that. I didn't call
It anything. It seemed then product
Of school, parents, missed excursions to parks
And ponds; I felt myself waiting to grow,
Faster than oaks, taller than oaks, and free

To find that sun-charmed island where all time
Leaps with activity and magic. Lack
Of light did not seem like the problem then.
The slow addition of rings to elm-trunks did.
And there I was, thin sapling almost lost
To blight each year—bronchitis, winter's other
Gift to sickly children—just sitting still
Among the congregation, ladies in mink
And rouge and hair so stiff with spray it held
A snowflake longer than velvet. Those flakes
Still melted long before the choir could sing
The Christmas hymns we'd strain to sing with them,
The only hymns I ever learned the words to;
I loved to watch the black print coming clear
As the pages flickered under flame-light
Like leaves take on sun-color, though maybe
I never thought of that. I'd like to think
I did. I'd like to think I knew so much
About God then, before I learned the shape
Of years, the seasons, whole forests lost to time
And, like lost faith, no getting past "hard fact"
And no winning the shortest-lost souls back.

The Drive

I don't know, some days my vision is different
When I'm riding up a long hill on Southwest 59
And suddenly nothing has ever been so
Beautiful as the rear ends of a dozen cars
Swaying from lane to lane ahead, some finding
Themselves blocked and dropping back,
Some darting through just-opened gaps,
Some grinding a steady pace in the right lane;
The sky is stitched with clouds and far away,
And we are all heading somewhere we hold
In the back of the mind, not thinking it
But pinning it there so we don't get lost
In our thoughts or the angled maze of exits
Branching off the main road and looping
Over like frozen vines, stiff enough to shatter.
From what we know of one another we are all
Heads and hands, lifting the lighter's circular
Coal to a cigarette, reaching to smooth back
Hair loosened by the a/c turned up high; I like
Being alone out there, driving too fast,
Keeping an eye out for cops. I sling my bags
In the passenger seat and look any direction
I want to. It's not like the nights six months ago
Before they finished this stretch of freeway;
The crews worked under lights and closed off
All but one lane. Traffic backed up for miles,
And more than once I got stuck there
With my husband after we'd been arguing.
Sometimes we'd been at it all day, not even
Stopping to eat, and now we'd be done in
For a while, not over it, just empty.
He'd call in an order at Kim So'n and I'd
Drive because I get there faster, but soon
As I'd register cruising speed I'd have to hit
The brakes and line up in the line of taillights
Slowed single-file past the workmen.
Some workers wrestled jackhammers,
Some drove trucks flashing yellow lights,

Some only seemed to be standing there
Breathing the clouds of concrete dust that drifted
Over the carpool lane, then made straight
For the stars. There was nothing to do
But watch them work, my husband and I,
Our jaws set, necks stiff as the hard pods
Rattlebox sprouts in roadside ditches;
He'd said before he had nothing to say,
And now I didn't either. Soon we'd inch close
To the part of town we lived in seven years
Ago, before we'd learned so little about
Love; I don't know what he was thinking,
But I was remembering walking the dog,
My husband and I, late at night in a park
Where on weekends couples met, some gay,
Others straight; boys of eighteen on bicycles
Rode around and around the same block.
The fountain boasted a broken obelisk,
A metal sculpture in the pool's shallow center;
One night when I'd been drinking too much
I rolled up my pants and took the dog in,
I clambered through the water and lured
The dog behind me, he barked because
He hated the water but he wanted to be
With me. My husband stood silent on the walk
At the pool's edge. He was nervous I'd get us
In trouble. "Be still," I knew he wanted to whisper.
"Don't make so much noise and let's go home."
He wasn't thinking I'd remember how
He looked, standing in front of a thicket
Of frizzy bamboo, hands in his pockets
And mouth set like a man working hard.
Those weeks the crews were paving the freeway
It might take an hour to get to Kim So'n,
And the hot and sour soup might be cold
When we got it home. I learned it was better
Not to mention that. I learned to like it
When we didn't speak, when he silently switched
On CNN and we watched the politicians. I learned it
Sometime alone, though, in daylight, changing
Lanes doing seventy and thinking about
The changes in me since I came to this place
Where you forget the seasons, you start to think

It's one long year since you first drove
Into town on 59 and cars coming close in the dark
Narrow lanes still scared you. It's easy to get lost
Like that, lost in your own thoughts,
Missing the scenery going by, though no one
Would call it beautiful, something always going up,
A highway widened, trucks crawling alongside;
It's all like that, it all looks the same.
You could get lost and not wander back,
You could speed up and chase the end of day.

Grown Women

She doesn't want to say the bad words.
She doesn't want to have the angry ideas.
She's living with a telephone lineman, his
Two kids from a previous marriage, and she had
One too; but labor drove her blood pressure up,
She could've had a stroke, and it took two days
To have her son after the water broke.
I've visited the town where they live, I don't
Call it a town, it's sandhill, shack, and farmland;
And I didn't see fences, but she doesn't roam.
We used to love one another. I don't know if
We felt desire. If we did, we lived it differently;
We had men to the house where we lived,
College friends, and passed in the hall late at night,
Wrapped in towels, our hair messed up from sex;
Maybe we felt embarrassed, we'd laugh, knowing
Those men weren't "right" for us. We knew
We were heading where good men would find us.

Where she lives the sun comes up over flatlands
Sowed with corn and tobacco. Where I live the sun
Comes up in a bowl of sky and burns like cherry
Candy for a short half-hour. I left the man I
Married. I tender my apology as I would to a tree
I'd bumped into; I couldn't really do damage
Like that, I go inside and take my clothes off
To check for bruises. In winter the deer strip
Bark from trunks, but it's plain peeled green
Underneath, delicate, not human. Now
The tallest treetops glitter, dampness has risen
From earth overnight and the sun will blot it away
Soon enough, but it's only the sun that lets me see it.
By the time I could face him, the man I married,
I told him I wanted a child, but it was too
Late. There was no money, no heart, no need
To touch except with words, those tiny twirling
Star-shaped knives like the weapons in karate
Movies. He loved to watch them. He read Freud

And Nietzsche until he was tired, then plugged
Cassettes into the VCR, and I smoked dope and sank
Into myself. What would a daughter be to him,
I worried. What would a son be. I knew about
Fairy rings in mown grass, I didn't know what caused
Them, I knew many people fear them, I didn't know
They never go away. I wanted a life in the balance,
I'd seen it depicted, bodies and dreams and nerves
And anger that vanished like a kiss. I mean
I found out the direction, I mean I swam
Close to the muddy bottom, I mean it was the top
And I was upside down. We've lived here so long
Beside these lakes, when you dive into them,
Everything we've thrown away is floating
Down there, tangled in what looks like sash cord,
Thin brown ropes of it, holding down exactly
The forgotten. It's true benevolence.

She knows what's tethered underwater. Not
Children's bodies, but their toys, their lost,
Lawed-against pleasures. I'm not going to
Take up with her the ways we were persuaded
To throw our joys into dark water. We might've
Thought we would cleanse them, they would bob
To the surface, slick as leaves. We were good
At happiness, and that defined us suspect, as
The forest is suspect, for the green fringe
Disguising the shadow; as the sea is suspect,
For the polished glass smoothing the sheer path
Down. Years ago, when we loved each other,
We used to take trips in her brother's beat-up
Cougar; the muffler knocked up sparks, dragging
The asphalt, the doors wouldn't shut quite flush,
The wind ruined our hair worse than jolting
Sex. I thought she was the more beautiful.
She thought I was the more beautiful.
We found highways leading deep into mountains,
Sometimes right through them, tunnels plated
With sea-green tiles, where the signs said
Turn on headlights, and that was the law,
To see for a minute or two before bursting back
Into strong sunlight and forgetting how it hides
The darkness, just masks it, really, so you can't

Know which side you're on, you end up taking it
For granted, and then, one day, when you ask
For what you want, someone says, it's too late,
It's all been taken, we're closing now,
You'll have to go home alone, don't come back.